Bokuden
AND THE
Bully

A
Japanese
Folktale

Adapted by STEPHEN KRENSKY

Illustrated by CHERYL KIRK NOLL

On My Own

FOLKLORE

Ⅲ Millbrook Press/Minneapolis

Special thanks to Yuiko Kimura, Associate Researcher, Department of Japanese and Korean Art, Minneapolis Institute of Arts, for serving as a consultant on this title

Millbrook Press
A division of Lerner Publishing Group, Inc.
241 First Avenue North
Minneapolis, MN 55401 U.S.A.

Website address: www.lernerbooks.com

Library of Congress Cataloging-in-Publication Data

Krensky, Stephen.
    Bokuden and the bully : a Japanese folktale / adapted by Stephen Krensky;
illustrated by Cheryl Kirk Noll.
       p.   cm. — (On my own folklore)
    Summary: Relates how Bokuden Tsukahara, the greatest swordsman of
sixteenth-century Japan, deals with a boastful, bullying warrior during a
ferry ride across a great river.
    ISBN: 978–0–8225–7547–4 (lib. bdg. : alk. paper)
    1. Tsukahara, Bokuden 16th cent.—Legends. [1. Tsukahara, Bokuden
16th cent.—Legends. 2. Folklore—Japan.] I. Noll, Cheryl Kirk, ill. II. Title.
PZ8.1.K8663Bok 2009
398.2—dc22   2007010046

Manufactured in the United States of America
2 3 4 5 6 7 – DP – 14 13 12 11 10 09

For Peter —S.K.

For Mom and Dad, with my love and gratitude —C.K.N.

Boarding the Ferry

Tsukahara Bokuden was
a great nobleman.
He was an even better swordsman.
And he was also curious
about the world.
Many times,
Bokuden left his home to travel.
He always wore simple clothes
to fit in with his fellow travelers.
But he also carried his sword,
because some places were dangerous
for a man traveling alone.
There was much to learn
from new people and places.
And Bokuden was eager to learn.

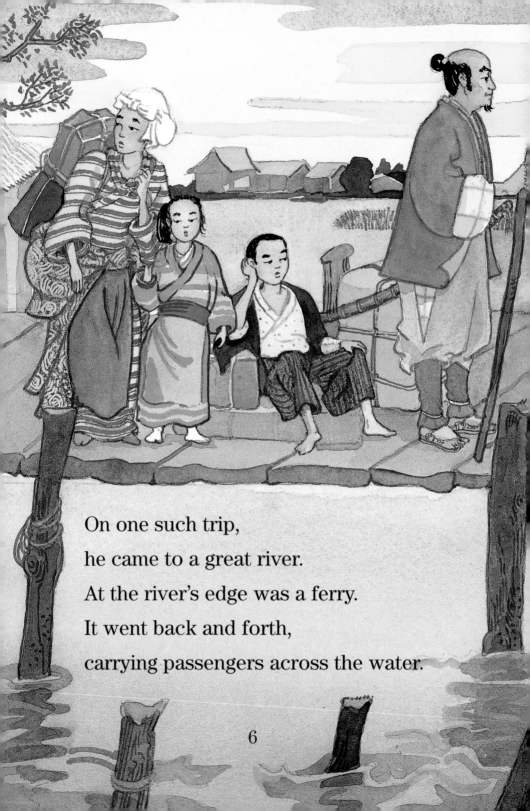

On one such trip,
he came to a great river.
At the river's edge was a ferry.
It went back and forth,
carrying passengers across the water.

6

People were standing in line
to buy tickets.
Bokuden waited his turn like everyone else.
Well, almost everyone.

A fierce warrior was trying
to push his way to the front.
He was a head taller than
everyone else—and a head wider too.

"Move aside," the warrior said.
He grabbed a peasant
by the shoulder.
"You are standing in my spot."
The peasant was surprised
at the warrior's manner.
"This is not your spot," he said.
"You have only just arrived."

"Exactly," said the warrior.

"And now that I am here,

I wish to stand where you are."

"That is not fair," said the peasant.

"I have waited here for an hour.

You are a soldier.

Should you not defend the law?"

"The law here is what I make it,"
said the warrior.
"As you say, I am a soldier.
Do you see the sword I am wearing?
Do you think I know how to use it?
I will be happy to demonstrate—
on you."

11

The peasant bowed deeply.

He could see that the warrior was not

listening to him.

"I am unarmed,

and I spoke without thinking.

Forgive me.

Please take my space."

"That's better," said the warrior.

"And since you are so proud

of standing in line, why don't you

go to the end and do it again."

The peasant, seeing no other choice,

did as he was told.

Crossing the River

Once all the tickets were sold,
the passengers boarded the ferry
for the trip over the water.

The day was bright, and Bokuden hoped to enjoy the fine weather.
He took a seat and closed his eyes.

15

Not far away, the fierce warrior
strutted around the deck.
"Move!" he said to a farmer
nearby.
"But I was here first,"
the farmer replied.
"Why does that matter?"
asked the warrior.
"This is where I wish to enjoy
the view.
Do you see the sword I am wearing?
Do you think I know how to use it?"
The farmer bowed deeply.
"I have no wish to fight over the view.
I will find another place."
And he scampered away.

A merchant in fine clothes
shook his head.

"That was not right," he said.

The warrior turned on him.

"Do you wish to make it right?"

"No, no," said the merchant,
turning pale.

"I am not dressed for the part."

"If I carve you up into little pieces,"
said the warrior, "it will not matter
how you are dressed."

The merchant gripped his soft shirt tightly.

"Forgive me," he said.

"I regret my words."

"If I were to cut out your tongue," said the
warrior, "you would never have to worry
about that again."

The merchant scuttled off
as fast as he could.

"All of you are like frightened
little chickens," the warrior announced.
"You should crawl back
into your nice safe eggs."

The other passengers began
to move away from the warrior.
Soon, only Bokuden remained.
His eyes stayed closed.
And he was very still.

The warrior took out his sword
and waved it through the air.
He sliced up and down,
left and right.
He jabbed and parried.
"Why are you all staring?" he asked.
"Does anyone else wish to say something?"

Two children raised their hands.

"Yes, what is it?" the warrior asked.

"Have you fought in many battles?"
asked one child.

The warrior nodded.

"Too many to count."

"Have you ever been wounded?"
asked the other child.
"I give wounds.
I do not receive them."
Someone snorted.
The warrior snapped around.
"Who was that?" he demanded.
No one spoke.

A Different Art

The warrior was not satisfied
with the silence.
"I will discover who has mocked me.
Whoever it is will pay
for his opinion."
Someone snorted again.
This time, the warrior walked up
to Bokuden.
He stared down at the nobleman.
"You there!" the warrior declared.
Bokuden's eyes were still closed.
"I am talking to you,"
said the warrior.
He poked the nobleman
in the shoulder.

Bokuden opened his eyes.

"I was having the most delightful dream," he said.

"I don't suppose you can tell me how it ends."

The warrior laughed harshly.

"I don't suppose I care.

You seem to have more backbone

than the rest of these worms.

What do you have to say

about my sword skills?"

"My apologies," said Bokuden.

"Did you put on a show?

I was not really paying attention."

"Pay attention NOW,"
said the warrior,
and he repeated his best moves.
When he was finished,
he turned back to Bokuden.
"What do you think of that?"
he asked.

"Very lively," said Bokuden.

"Lively!" cried the warrior.

"Why, not one swordsman in
one hundred can claim such skill."

Bokuden looked around.

"Since one hundred swordsmen are not here,
I will have to take your word for that."

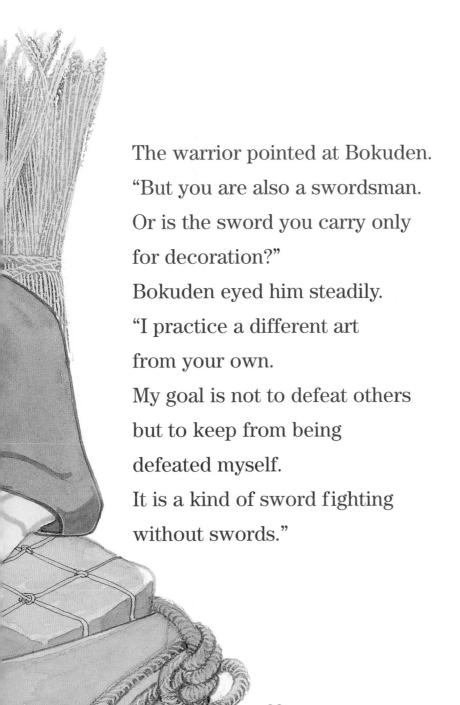

The warrior pointed at Bokuden.
"But you are also a swordsman.
Or is the sword you carry only
for decoration?"
Bokuden eyed him steadily.
"I practice a different art
from your own.
My goal is not to defeat others
but to keep from being
defeated myself.
It is a kind of sword fighting
without swords."

The warrior laughed.

"I have never heard of such a thing.

Has this art served you well?"

Bokuden opened his arms wide.

"So far it has."

The warrior laughed again.

"I would like to see

this sword fighting

without swords."

"Very well," said Bokuden.

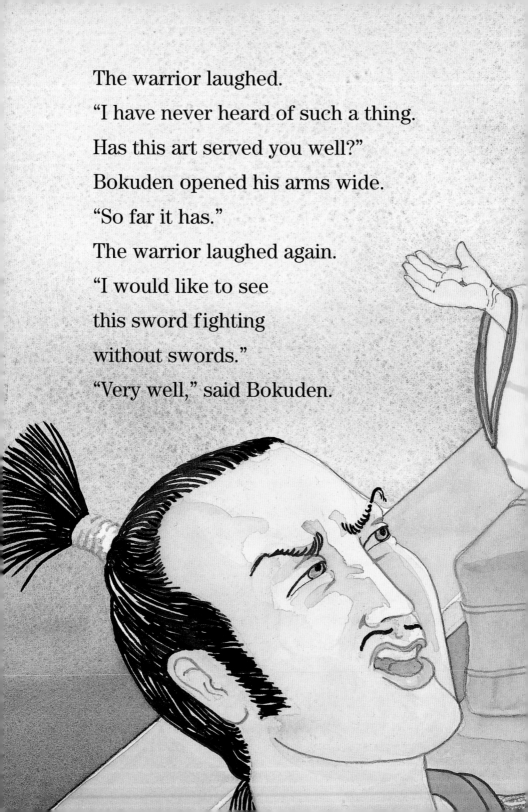

Bokuden looked around.

"Here on the ferry, there is not enough room

for a proper contest.

Let us take one of the rowboats

to that island."

He pointed over the bow.

"There we will have enough space
to move around."
The warrior agreed.
As a crowd gathered to watch,
Bokuden and the warrior
rowed away together.

Fighting with One Sword

Bokuden and the warrior
reached the island.
Then the warrior jumped out
of the boat onto the shore.
He could not wait
for the contest to begin.
Right away,
he began waving his sword.

The blade flashed in the sunlight.

On board the ferry,

the passengers were amazed.

The warrior was truly a fierce fighter.

His sword flashed like lightning.

What chance did the quiet stranger have

against him?

The warrior was thinking much
the same thing.
But he had failed to notice something.
Bokuden had not followed him
onto the shore.

He was still sitting in the boat.
"Hurry up," the warrior demanded.
"I do not expect this to take long.
I cannot promise to be merciful,
but I will be quick."

In answer, Bokuden put his oar
back in the water.
"Where are you going?"
the warrior shouted.
"Back to the ferry,"
Bokuden answered.
The warrior laughed harshly.
"But we have not fought yet.
Are you really such a coward?"
"Tsukahara Bokuden
is many things," said Bokuden.
"Perhaps not all of them
are worthy of praise.
But never has he been called
a coward."

The crowd aboard the ferry gasped.
Tsukahara Bokuden was the greatest
swordsman in all of Japan.
If he would not fight this
boastful warrior, it could only be
to save the poor man's life.

44

"This is what is called sword fighting without swords," Bokuden went on. "And unless you are as great a swimmer as you are a warrior, we are done with your first lesson." Leaving the warrior shaking his fist, Bokuden rowed away.

Afterword

© Diane Skoss/Koryu Books

This folktale is about a real person, Tsukahara Bokuden. Bokuden lived in Japan from 1489 to 1571. He was adopted into a noble family. His father taught him a kind of martial arts called *Tenshin Shoden Katori Shinto-ryo* that focused on swordplay. As he grew older, Bokuden traveled all over Japan to learn from the most skilled swordsmen. He liked to travel in search of adventure, and he often found it. Bokuden started the kashima style of fencing, *Kashima Shinto-ryu*. He was called a kensei, a "sword saint."

Bokuden became so well known and admired that people began to tell stories about him. Storytellers used these tales to teach lessons. In this folktale, a rude and arrogant warrior challenges Bokuden. Instead of answering the warrior with more rudeness, Bokuden shows grace and a sense of humor. Like other folktales told all over the world, the hero wins by being smarter, not stronger or faster, than the villain.

Glossary

bow: the front of a boat

coward: someone who is afraid of many things

ferry: a boat that carries people across a body of water, such as a river or a lake

jab: to stab or poke quickly

merchant: a trader, someone who buys a product then sells it for profit

merciful: kind or compassionate

mocked: made fun of in a mean way

nobleman: an aristocrat or person in the upper class

parry: to push a weapon away, protecting oneself

passenger: a traveler who pays to be carried from one place to another

peasant: someone who works on a farm, usually uneducated and lower class

swordsman: someone who is skilled at the art of handling a sword

warrior: someone who has fought in a battle

wounded: injured or hurt

Further Reading and Websites

Books

Iedwab, Claudio A. *The Peaceful Way: A Children's Guide to the Traditions of the Martial Arts.* Rochester, VT: Destiny Books, 2001. This book shows that martial arts are not about fighting. They are about resolving conflict in life. It shows that by cultivating a positive attitude of humility, honesty, awareness, and discipline, the martial arts student learns both physical and mental focus.

Kimmel, Eric A. *Sword of the Samurai: Adventure Stories from Japan.* San Diego: Harcourt Brace, 1999. This collection of eleven stories introduces the swordsmen and women who reigned in Japan for more than 1200 years.

Littlefield, Holly. *Colors of Japan.* Minneapolis: Carolrhoda Books, 1997. This picture book uses colors to illustrate Japanese culture.

Scandiffio, Laura. *The Martial Arts Book.* Toronto: Annick Press, 2003. This book introduces the spiritual aspects of martial arts as well as the history of the major branches. It also shows the ways that judo and tai chi, among other branches, have moved from ancient times into the present and from Asia into the West.

Website

Ninjutsu.at: Tsukahara Bokuden
http://www.ninjutsu.at/index.php?option=com_content&task=view&id=72&Itemid=30
This website tells two tales about Tsukahara Bokuden.